Original title:

Marigold Musings

Author: Cameron Blair

ISBN HARDBACK: 978-1-80566-641-7

ISBN PAPERBACK: 978-1-80566-926-5

Warm Embrace of Color

In gardens bright, where colors play,
A bee steals nectar and flies away.
With pollen pants and cheerful cheer,
They buzz and hum, always near.

The flowers giggle as they sway,
Each petal whispers, 'Come, let's play!'
A clown in bloom, oh what a sight,
Dancing in the warm sunlight.

Reflections in Bloom

A daisy pranced, all dressed in white,
She fancied herself a dazzling sight.
The tulips laughed, their heads held proud,
'You're just a dot,' they sang out loud.

In puddles formed from last night's rain,
The blooms reflected, 'We're dancing again!'
A splash of color, the petals shout,
'Hey, look at us! We're in, no doubt!'

Sun-Kissed Thoughts

The sun stretched wide upon the ground,
While flowers giggled, look how they've browned!
A thought occurred, 'Don't tan too much!'
The daisies blushed—'It's just a touch.'

With scents so sweet, the butterflies came,
They played tag, oh what a game!
While sipping nectar with silly grins,
They crowded close and joined the spins.

The Embrace of Light

A sunflower stretched, reaching up high,
It tried to touch the clouds in the sky.
The clouds just chuckled, 'You're aiming wrong!'
'We can't play catch, you don't belong.'

But with each ray, they danced with glee,
The shadows played, so wild and free.
In a flash of golden, the day looks bright,
Nature's jesters, oh what delight!

A Tapestry of Sun

In fields of gold where petals sway,
The bees just buzz, they think they play.
With no concerns of time or place,
They dance around in buzzing grace.

The wise old owl looks down with glee,
"Just take a break and enjoy the spree!"
But all the flowers start to bloom,
And that just makes a noisy room.

The ladybugs wear spots with pride,
They strut about, their hearts so wide.
While ants parade in single file,
Except when one trips—watch him smile!

Oh, cotton clouds in skies so blue,
They chuckle down to come join too.
In this circus, nature's show,
Where laughter's found among the glow.

The Glow of Nature's Heart

Underneath the bright sun's glow,
A squirrel spins in quite a show.
He leaps and lands, makes quite a splash,
While onlookers gather, giggle, and dash.

The flowers chat, they spill their tea,
And gossip 'bout the bumblebee.
"Did you hear he crashed in the pond?"
"Oh dear, I really must be fond!"

A butterfly flutters, with flair and style,
She twirls in the air, adding a smile.
With her delicate wings, a bright delight,
Poised for a dance, she takes off in flight.

The sun dips low, what a quirky sight,
As critters prepare for the calm of night.
With twinkling stars, they switch the theme,
And all join hands for the moonlit dream.

Colorful Reverberations

In gardens bright with hues galore,
The colors clash, they laugh and roar.
From purple pansies to red carnations,
They hold wild parties with no relation.

The tulips sing in perfect tune,
While sunlight dips behind the moon.
They strut in style, with petals puffed,
Believing they're the absolute stuffed.

Charming daisies, white and bold,
Tell jokes that never grow old.
They titter and giggle, a funny sight,
As bees with grins buzz through the night.

The vibrant hues, a glorious mess,
Join together, they simply bless.
They're a lively crew, oh, what a scene,
Laughing and swirling, the best you've seen!

Garden of Dreams

In the garden where flowers play,
The daisies dance and sway.
Butterflies wear tiny shoes,
While snoozing ants sip morning brews.

The sun sneezes, clouds all flee,
Bumblebees sing off-key.
The carrots giggle in their patch,
While radishes plan a funny match.

Tulips tell the best of tales,
While peonies sneak out on sails.
In this world, all's a jest,
Where even weeds know how to rest.

So come along, don't be late,
This garden's truly first-rate.
With blooms that laugh and brightly cheer,
A place where joy is always near.

Light in Bloom

In the glow where colors burst,
Laughter comes, we're feeling versed.
A sunflower wears a hat so tall,
While daisies giggle, having a ball.

The bees are busy, buzzing loud,
With pollen suits, they feel so proud.
A single tulip starts to sway,
Its secret? Dance like there's no way!

The garden gnome tells jokes all day,
His best friend, a snail, joins the fray.
While ladybugs form a band,
They twirl and spin, oh isn't it grand?

With every petal, laughter blooms,
In this bright land where joy consumes.
So come and play beneath the sun,
In this garden where we all have fun.

Seeds of Sunshine

Tiny seeds in rows so neat,
Dream of dancing on their feet.
The tomatoes wear shades, oh so bright,
While pumpkins giggle, it's quite the sight.

In dirt, the worms play jump rope,
With radishes cheering, "We'll help you cope!"
With every sprout, a laugh is shared,
These sunny seeds, they must be spared.

Sprinklers giggle as they spray,
Making rainbows in the day.
And cheerful crows croon silly rhymes,
They've got style — for bird-chasing times!

So plant a smile, let laughter grow,
In this quirky garden flow.
With seeds of sunshine, come join the show,
In this wacky world where joy will glow.

The Heart of the Garden

At the heart where blossoms dream,
Petals swirl like whipped cream.
The orchids prance, they take the lead,
While geraniums plot a comical deed.

A mischievous sprout plays hide-and-seek,
With tulips shouting, "We're far too chic!"
While pansies giggle at the weeds,
Their jokes are planted with clever seeds.

Bumblebees wear tiny capes,
As wind carries laughter in drapes.
And frogs croak out a chorus loud,
Inviting all to join the crowd.

This garden grins from root to tip,
In every bud, a laughter sip.
So take your time, enjoy the fun,
In the heart of this garden, happiness is spun.

Golden Whispers in the Garden

In the garden, whispers glow,
Plants gossip as breezes flow.
A bee wears goggles, so absurd,
While butterflies dance, undeterred.

The sun winks at a lazy cat,
Who contemplates a chirping spat.
Flowers giggle, heads held high,
As grasshoppers plan their next skyfly.

Worms in suits are plotting schemes,
To sell their soil in fragrant dreams.
On daisies' heads, a tiny crown,
Swaying gently, never down.

Frogs host concerts on lily pads,
While snails wear bows, oh what fads!
Every corner, joy abounds,
In the laughter that surrounds.

Petals of Daydreams

Petals flutter, tales untold,
Of a baker who bakes in gold.
His bread does dance, it's quite a sight,
While seeds plot mischief late at night.

Bees wear top hats, oh so spry,
As daisies twirl beneath the sky.
A caterpillar sips his tea,
While claiming he's a VIP.

Squirrels in tuxedos gather round,
For a ball where jokes abound.
They juggle acorns, make us laugh,
While worms debate the craft of math.

With giggles shared on every leaf,
Nature thrives in joyful grief.
These daydreams float like puffy clouds,
In a garden full of giggly crowds.

Echoes of Autumn Hues

Leaves spin tales in colors bright,
Dancing freely in golden light.
A pumpkin sings in quirky tones,
While critters shuffle with their phones.

Squirrels plan a nutty parade,
Debating which tree to invade.
A crow cracks jokes atop a post,
While woodpeckers drum, they love to boast.

Acorns roll and start a race,
Chasing shadows, quicken pace.
A hedgehog dons a scarf so grand,
With elbows out, he takes a stand.

In this burst of autumn cheer,
Every laugh we hold so dear.
Echoes linger, soft and bright,
In the whimsical autumn light.

Sunlit Serenade Unfolds

In sunlit fields, a show begins,
Where daisies chuckle, laughter spins.
Grass tickles toes, oh what a prank,
As butterflies dance along the bank.

A sunflower winks in golden grace,
While shadows play a game of chase.
Crickets chirp their evening tune,
While frogs croak loud, beneath the moon.

Bumblebees buzz with jokes galore,
In a hive that's never a bore.
A ladybug dons a tiny hat,
While ants serve tea, oh how about that!

With every petal, joy prevails,
In stories spun by whimsy trails.
Sunlit serenade, a grand delight,
In nature's warmth, we find our light.

Sunkissed Reflections

Golden blooms in summer's race,
Dancing petals, such a face.
They giggle when the breeze hits right,
Waving at the bees in flight.

A bee in shades, how very fly,
Buzzing tunes as clouds drift by.
With nectar dreams they start to scheme,
Caught in a sweet, sticky dream.

Sunshine sneezes, flowers laugh,
Nature's joy, a silly craft.
Petals blushing, oh so bright,
Rolling in the warm sunlight.

Laughter floats on sunny air,
Petal pranks we cannot spare.
Sunkissed moments, oh so fine,
Living life like wine and dine.

The Spirit of Sunshine

Laughing petals stretch so wide,
Waving hands from side to side.
Sunshine's spirit, bright and bold,
Telling jokes that never get old.

Dandelions in a wind race,
Chasing shadows, sprightly pace.
With pollen jokes, they spread the cheer,
Humming tunes for all to hear.

Bumblebees join in the game,
Buzzing laughter, never tame.
Sipping sunshine, oh so sweet,
Life in blooms, a funny treat.

Sunflares wiggle in delight,
Making flowers bloom with might.
In the garden, joy takes flight,
Painting life in colors bright.

Following the Sunlight

Chasing rays, a cheery quest,
Little blooms know they are blessed.
Following sunlight, oh, what fun,
Growing tall to greet the sun.

In their hats, the daisies sway,
With each breeze, they dance and play.
Sunshine tickles, laughter swells,
Garden stories, who can tell?

With every grin, a petal blush,
Competing in a happy rush.
Giggling as the sun rolls high,
In this field, we can't be shy.

Each golden hour, smiles parade,
Life's a silly serenade.
In the warmth, absurdity,
Joining blooms in harmony.

Hues of Happiness

Orange and yellow in a spread,
Petals painting joy instead.
Dancing colors, bold and bright,
Creating smiles, sheer delight.

Amidst the laughter, a tussle falls,
Sunhats flying, oh, the calls.
Tickled by the playful breeze,
Petals shimmy with such ease.

Jokes exchanged with bumblebuns,
Time to shine, let's have some funs.
Each color dance, a silly flair,
Bringing happiness everywhere.

So here we sit, in hues so bright,
Lathered in love, pure sunlight.
Colorful antics, every day,
In the garden's joyful play.

Revelations in Soft Petals

In gardens where the sunbeams play,
Petals twirl in a silly display.
The bees chatter gossip, oh so bright,
While ants do the cha-cha, what a sight!

With every bloom, a secret to keep,
The flowers giggle, then fall asleep.
A butterfly trips on its own wing,
And the daisies laugh at the joy they bring.

Nature's Golden Intrigue

Gold dust glimmers in the summer's glow,
As squirrels tumble with a sprightly show.
The wind whispers, 'What's that in the air?'
A dandelion's wig floats without a care!

Frogs croak puns from their pondy throne,
While gophers dig holes with a cheerful tone.
Nature's jesters in cap and gown,
Making mischief all around town!

Blooms of Joy Underfoot

Step lightly on the petals below,
Each crunch is music to the ears, you know.
A hedgehog giggles, rolling with glee,
While snails hold a race, so slow but free!

The flowers cheer for each bumblebee,
Trying to woo a pretty pink tree.
With every step, a laughter resounds,
In this patch of joy, pure fun abounds!

Whispers from the Flowering Fields

Whispers float on a breezy tune,
The daisies plot under the light of the moon.
With a wink and a nod, they share their schemes,
Of tickling feet with their fragrant dreams!

Laughter sways in the summer's embrace,
While butterflies dance in a silly race.
Fields of colors burst into glee,
As flowers giggle, 'Come join our spree!'

Fields of Euphoria

In fields where giggles play,
The flowers dance and sway.
A bunny hops, a squirrel grins,
Nature's laughter softly spins.

The bees join in the fun,
Buzzing, oh so far they run.
Chasing shadows, what a sight,
Flower crowns worn, oh so light.

A dandelion's wish in tow,
Puffed out dreams begin to flow.
The breeze is tickling my nose,
As petals drop in silly throws.

Clouds above are cotton candy,
Life's a joke, oh so dandy!
With a sprinkle of sunshine,
In this field, all's divine.

Sun-Kissed Whispers

Beneath the sun, a muffin laughs,
With berries on its fluffy halves.
A ladybug takes a ride,
On a fern that's full of pride.

The flowers wear their brightest hues,
Chatting gossip, sharing news.
A quirky chat among the blooms,
While pollen dances 'neath the fumes.

The sun's warm kiss is quite the tease,
As daisies giggle in the breeze.
With blossoms buzzing silly tunes,
And butterflies on blinking moons.

Oh, the petals prance with glee,
In this garden, wild and free!
With chuckles, laughter fills the air,
A sunny space with joy to share.

Floral Daydreams

In dreamland where the petals play,
Silly thoughts are here to stay.
A daffodil in party shoes,
Twirling in its golden hues.

The roses tease with fragrance sweet,
Joking that they're quite the treat.
While tulips boast their colors bright,
Competing for the day's spotlight.

The daisies laugh with cheeky grace,
As lily pads join the race.
A butterfly slips on a shoe,
Twirling 'round, what a view!

Between the petals, secrets hide,
While bees and blooms glide side by side.
In floral dreams, the jokes are grand,
A whimsical, enchanted land.

Gold-Flaked Reverie

In a garden full of cheer,
The grasshoppers sing loud and clear.
A sunflower tips its hat,
While a nearby toad looks quite fat.

With petals like gold, the laughter rolls,
As bumblebees perform their trolls.
A rose did trip, with style and flair,
While violets giggle without a care.

The wind spins tales through branches bare,
Echoed back by blooms so rare.
A gecko winks, then scampers by,
Pretending he can touch the sky.

Oh, in this reverie of light,
Even shadows dance in delight.
With every giggle, we all agree,
Nature's jest—what a jubilee!

The Language of Blooms

In the garden where flowers chat,
Roses throw shade, just like a cat.
Daisies gossip, not a care,
Tulips pose with the breezy air.

Petunias giggle, what a sight,
Sunflowers shush at a nearby light.
Lilies wink with pollen gold,
While pansies tell tales, brave and bold.

The violets tease, all in good fun,
While the bees buzz loudly, on the run.
With petals swirling, laughter flies,
Nature holds a comical guise.

So next time you wander, take a glance,
These floral friends love to prance.
In their world of colors, bright and free,
Every bloom speaks with glee, you'll see!

Sunflower Shadows

In fields where sunflowers make a stand,
They nod to each other, a silly band.
With faces that turn for a sunny tease,
Tickled by whispers of a light breeze.

Their stalks keep joking, they'll never bend,
Blooming with laughter until the end.
Petal pouts when clouds block the fun,
"Hey, sunshine, hurry! We've just begun!"

They wear yellow hats with a twist so fine,
Dancing in shadows, a comical line.
Swaying like dancers, they steal the show,
Each sunflower thinking it's a Picasso glow.

So come join their game, leave worries behind,
In the humor of petals, endless you'll find.
With a smile as bright as the noon-time glow,
Sunflower shadows steal the show!

Vibrant Glimmers

In a patch of colors, oh what a tease,
Buttercups giggle with buzzing bees.
Bluebells chime in with a jolly sound,
As daisies do a dance all around.

Zinnias jump, 'Look at our flair!'
While poppies laugh, they just don't care.
Every petal's a party, a jubilant spree,
Nature's own riot, wild and free.

When the moon flirts and stars take stage,
Plants share secrets as they engage.
With twinkling giggles, they light the night,
In joyful harmony, a sheer delight.

So pause among blooms, let laughter ignite,
In their vibrant glimmers, hearts feel light.
Where flowers plus fun, the ripple is grand,
Join in their revel and you'll understand!

Whispers of the Meadow

In the meadow where wild things play,
Petals whisper secrets of the day.
Grasshoppers chirp, what a silly crew,
Even gentle breezes join in too!

A clover giggles at the buzzing flies,
While the daisies wink with mischievous eyes.
Butterflies flit, creating a mess,
More drama than any daytime press!

"Why did the flower break up?" asks sage,
"Because it found another bouquet!"
The lilies chuckle, hidden in green,
Every petal knows, laughter's their scene.

So stroll through the meadow, share a good laugh,
In the whispers of petals, they'll share their craft.
With the sunshine above and joy all around,
In the whims of the flowers, true fun is found!

Joyful Petal Ponderings

In a garden of giggles, they sway,
Petals chatting all night and day.
Sunshine tickles, blossoms beam,
Laughter blooms, a floral dream.

Worms in tuxedos take a spin,
Joking with roots, where do we begin?
Bees with sunglasses, buzzing in style,
They dance and prance, all the while.

Rabbits hop by with silly hats,
Fluffy and funny, where's the chitchat?
They sip on dew from a tiny cup,
Enjoying the joy of nature's ups.

And when the moon starts to glow,
Petals whisper secrets soft and low.
A waltz of petals, a jolly affair,
In this garden of laughter, no room for despair.

Bright Horizons

Under bright skies, the flowers do cheer,
Planting jokes for everyone near.
With every breeze, their stories dart,
Creating a canvas for laughter's art.

Sunflowers giggle, swinging wide,
Telling tales of the bugs that hide.
Daisies chime in, the fun they spread,
Silly anecdotes of a snail they dread.

Butterflies waltz, with grace they glide,
On a quest for nectar, they take a ride.
"Why did the flower join a band?" they tease,
"Because it had the best roots for a breeze!"

In these bright horizons, humor flows,
Among happy blooms, the laughter grows.
Each petal a punchline, each stem a glee,
In this garden of smiles, come share with me!

Glistening Leaf Tales

Leaves whisper secrets, shiny and bright,
In the cool shade, they share delight.
What did one leaf say to the other?
"Stop being so shady, let's find a brother!"

Raindrops giggle, splashing about,
Puddles reflecting the fun, no doubt.
Each drop a dancer, no one fell flat,
Just splish and splash, oh what's up with that?

Squirrels indulge in a nutty chat,
"Why visit the tree that's losing its hat?"
A great bark of laughter echoes nearby,
In this leafy world, they spread joy high.

As sunlight dapples, igniting the trees,
Nature mutters jokes on the sweetest breeze.
With each rustle, the hilarity sails,
Gather 'round friends for glistening leaf tales.

Dance of the Marigold

Under the sun, the colors collide,
A whimsical dance that can't be denied.
Each marigold twirls, a sight to behold,
Spinning and laughing, defying the cold.

"Why can't you trust a flower?" they say,
"Because they always seem to sway!"
With roots in the ground, and heads held high,
They chuckle and bounce, oh my, oh my!

Ladybugs join in, beats on the ground,
With silly little steps, they prance around.
"Let's have a party!" the petals do shout,
In a festival of blooms, there's no room for doubt.

So join the fun, let your worries unfold,
In the vibrant chaos, let joy be consoled.
With every dance, life's laughter enrolls,
Together we'll bloom, as the marigold rolls.

A Tapestry of Sunlit Days

In the garden where laughter blooms,
Dancing gnomes chase away the glooms.
Sunshine spills like lemonade,
Tickling toes in the grassy parade.

Bumblebees buzz with gossip so sweet,
While ants hold a picnic, oh what a feat!
Squirrels wear hats, yes it's a riot,
Nature's own circus, and we can't deny it.

Butterflies with antics so grand,
Flap their wings, slip from the planned.
They flutter and tumble, what a sight,
I'm sure they're partying all through the night.

So join in the fun, don a big grin,
Laughter is sunshine, let the day begin!
In this tapestry of joyful play,
Every heart blooms brighter, come what may.

The Beauty of Gentle Radiance

Oh, look at the flowers, they jive and sway,
Trying to dance, but they've lost their way.
Petals flapping like an old man's scarf,
Caught in the breeze, let's hear them laugh!

The sun wears shades, what a funny sight,
While birds serenade the morning light.
A cat in a sunbeam, oh what a tease,
Chasing its tail like it's a big cheese!

They say the daisies have secrets to share,
But they giggle and hide under foliage there.
They wave their heads, oh such mischief,
While the tulips gossip, growing stiff!

Life's a comedy, in colors so bright,
With each blossom smiling, pure delight.
So in this garden, let's cheer and play,
For the blooms bring joy in their own quirky way.

Sun-Kissed Memories Resound

Once I saw a sunflower wear a hat,
A jaunty, floppy, oversized spat.
It swayed and strutted with such grand flair,
A fashion show that none could compare!

Dandelions puff like tiny clouds,
Pretending to be kings, oh how proud!
They laugh when the breeze makes them spin,
Counting their wishes, let the fun begin!

Garden gnomes having a tea time so fine,
Brewing up joy, feeling divine.
With cookies made of dirt and moss,
Each bite is delicious, no need for gloss!

So here's to moments that tickle the soul,
Where laughter and petals take their stroll.
Captured in sunshine, let's spread the sound,
With each sun-kissed memory, joy is abound.

Petals that Brush the Sky

In a world where petals prank and tease,
They tickle the clouds, dance with the breeze.
A lily wore sneakers, can you believe?
Sprinting through gardens, oh what a reprieve!

Tiny fawns leap over daisies' heads,
While giggling butterflies giggle in beds.
The tulips whisper tales of grand flights,
Of chasing the sun through enchanting nights.

A bee stole a cupcake, ran like the wind,
While flowers join hands, a cute little band.
They sing whimsical tunes, soft and sweet,
In this garden party, there's no defeat!

So come one, come all, let laughter abide,
The petals are playful, with joy as our guide.
Let's make this moment, funny and spry,
For life's a delight when petals brush the sky!

Harvest of Warmth

In the garden, I found a bug,
Wearing a hat and a tiny rug.
He danced around with such delight,
Sipping nectar from dawn to night.

The sunflowers laughed, so tall and grand,
While bees drummed tunes in the warm land.
A scarecrow joined with a goofy pose,
Pretending he was a rockstar, who knows?

I tried to plant my veggies neat,
But found my shovel had gone to sleep.
With soil on my face, I stood in awe,
As rabbits bounced by, just to guffaw.

Yet through the chaos, joy springs free,
A harvest of giggles, you see!
In every leaf and sunny laugh,
Life's garden is a funny craft.

Golden Threads of Time

Golden threads weave tales so bright,
Of silly squirrels chasing their fright.
Each stitch a moment, each knot a tease,
Time's fabric tickles like a gentle breeze.

The clock giggles as it ticks away,
While my coffee's gone cold; oh, what a play!
I trip over memories, bright like gold,
In this wild tapestry, stories unfold.

A cat with a crown on its fuzzy head,
Claims the throne on my pillow, instead!
Meanwhile, a dog plays catch with his tail,
While laughter echoes like a merry whale.

As I stitch my days with glee and cheer,
I find humor lines stitched year by year.
In every moment, the joy will climb,
Life's golden threads create a rhyme.

Sunbeam Reflections

Sunbeams dance on the kitchen floor,
Where pancakes flip and giggle some more.
I chase my shadow; it runs away,
Leaving me laughing at the light of day.

The toaster pops with a sudden cheer,
As crumbs get scattered, oh dear, oh dear!
A whisk winks, as flour clouds rise,
In this bright kitchen, I wear my disguise.

The cat perches high with a regal smirk,
Watching my antics, it's quite the work.
It yawns with boredom as I lose control,
Baking this cake is taking a toll!

Yet in the mess, sunbeams shine bright,
Turning my chaos into pure delight.
With grins and giggles, I dare to reflect,
Moments of joy that I truly respect.

Petal Pathways

On pathways of petals, I stroll so light,
Dodging the puddles, with all my might.
Bumblebees buzz with a comical jest,
While skipping along, feeling truly blessed.

A ladybug stops with a wink and a nod,
As if proclaiming it's the best pod!
We share a giggle at the ants down below,
Marching in line, putting on a show.

A butterfly flutters in a dazzling dance,
Inviting me over for a chance romance.
But I trip on a vine and tumble down fast,
Making the petals giggle, what a blast!

Yet through it all, joy blooms so free,
In these silly moments, who wouldn't agree?
Pathways of petals lead me through grace,
With laughter and fun, there's always a place.

The Glitter of Garden Dreams

In a garden full of glee,
Worms wiggle like they're on TV.
Bees gossip while they sip and hum,
Petals dance to the buzzing drum.

Frogs croak while they scheme and plot,
With tadpole tailors, who'd have thought?
Rabbits munching on their leafy spoons,
Planning parties under the moons.

Ladybugs in their polka-dot suits,
Holding meetings on sunbeam routes.
They chat about the weather woes,
As snails race, but nobody knows.

Butterflies toss confetti flies,
While ants march by with cookies and pies.
In this garden, laughter's the theme,
Oh, the splendid charm of a dream!

Warm Embrace of Nature

In the woods where laughter grows,
Squirrels share their nutty prose.
Accidentally starting a feud,
Over who has the freshest food.

Trees whisper secrets, twist and sway,
While a raccoon steals the show today.
With costumes made from fallen leaves,
Dancing under, dreaming of thieves.

Hedgehogs in hats, so terribly bright,
Debating who snores louder at night.
Owls hoot while they sip their tea,
Critiquing pinecones — a fine degree!

The wind chuckles, tickles the grass,
As ants parade, they hope to amass.
With nature's quirks, each day's a play,
In this warm embrace, we hop and sway!

Captured Light

Sunbeams trap the squirrel crew,
Casting shadows, oh what a view!
Capacity for fun, they reign,
In this moment, free of disdain.

A feather floats and lands quite shy,
While crickets hum their lullaby.
A dandelion's wish spills away,
Blowing dreams where they may stay.

Butterflies flaunt their painted wings,
Competing for the brightest bling.
Chasing rays till the day is done,
In this captured light, we all run.

Fireflies blink a fleeting tease,
While sparrows gossip in bending trees.
Life is a laugh amidst the bright,
In the magic of captured light!

Woven with Gold

In a meadow stitched with sunshine,
Buzzing bees do ballet just fine.
With wildflowers as the stage,
Dancing sweetly, turning the page.

Bunnies jump like they've lost their wits,
While busy ants carry nutty bits.
Grasshoppers boast of leaps in the air,
Creating a ruckus without a care.

The wind tells tales of summer's delight,
As butterflies twirl, oh what a sight!
In this fabric of life, joy unfolds,
Every thread woven bright, gleaming like gold!

So let's gather in this playful spree,
Where nature's magic is ever free.
In laughter and light, we'll simply be,
Woven together, you and me!

Petals and Poetry

In a garden filled with cheer,
Petals dance without a fear.
Bees buzz by with silly grins,
While flowers giggle through their skins.

A flower claimed it won a race,
Against a snail with a proud face.
But as they stood to take a bow,
The wind knocked them both on a cow!

Daffodils wore hats of green,
Said, "Spring is here! Let's cause a scene!"
But daisies rolled their eyes and sighed,
"Can't you see? Our petals dried!"

So they laughed, and sang a tune,
While a ladybug joined soon.
In this patch of pure delight,
Every bloom was out of sight!

The Sun's Warm Touch

The sun peeked in, it's quite a tease,
It tickled leaves and swayed the trees.
A sunflower tilted for a chat,
With a lazy bumblebee named Pat.

"Hey there, buddy, what's the buzz?"
"Just soaking rays, oh what a fuzz!"
But then a cloud, with a frown so loud,
Blocked the sun, and the flowers bowed.

A rose complained, "This just ain't fair!
I need my tan, my sun-kissed hair!"
Yet when the rain came pouring down,
They all just danced without a frown.

So here's to warmth, and silliness,
To golden rays and flower bliss.
With every twist in nature's game,
This garden life will never tame!

Waking up with the Blossoms

As morning yawns and stretches wide,
The blossoms grin, they cannot hide.
A sleepy bud stumbles on its toes,
Then trips and lands on friends in rows.

"Oh, wake up, petals! Time to play!
The sun has painted all of May!"
A tulip sneezed, the pollen flew,
And soon the bees were buzzing too.

A daisy said, "Let's start a fight,
With a mud pie—what a delight!"
But violets giggled, "Let's instead
Snack on dew drops, then hop in bed!"

So they danced and twirled in light,
In this folly, oh what a sight!
Who knew that blossoms loved to play,
As morning outlined their bouquet?

Yellow Bliss

There once was a field, bright and bold,
Filled with yellow, or so I was told.
But when I peeked, oh what a jest,
It was just dandelions in a quest!

They wore their crowns, so proud and free,
Challenging tulips to a tea spree.
"Take a seat, let's don our best hats,
While we make friends with the nearby cats!"

The daisies cheered, and the lilies twirled,
In this crazy flowery world.
But when the wind zoomed by with glee,
It knocked off their hats—it was quite the spree!

Yet every bloom just laughed aloud,
In their yellow dresses, they felt so proud.
So if you see a flower's bliss,
Know they've had their fun, and you've missed!

The Light of Each New Dawn

In the morning light, I wake with grace,
My hair is a mess, I've lost the race.
Coffee in hand, I trip on my shoe,
Laughing out loud, it's the best thing to do.

Waking up early, what a big deal,
Socks mismatched, oh, how I feel!
Birds chirping sweet, yet I'm still in bed,
Dreaming of pastries dancing in my head.

Sunbeams peek in, my cat gives a yawn,
Chasing his tail, what a comical dawn!
I grin at the chaos, it brings me delight,
Every new morning is a wacky flight.

So let's raise a cup, here's to each morn,
With giggles and hiccups, let's keep our charm!
For in every sunrise, there's laughter to find,
Just like my coffee—sweet, light, and unlined.

A Journey Through Golden Fields

Strolling through fields of gold today,
I stepped on a slug and shouted, 'Hooray!'
With flowers a-bloom and bugs buzzing near,
Who knew nature had such a sense of cheer?

The sun on my back, the bugs in my hair,
I danced with a scarecrow, without a care.
Twirling and laughing, I flailed with glee,
Who knew farm life could be so free?

A butterfly perched on my nose, what a trick!
It fluttered away, I laughed till I'm sick.
The daisies agreed with their silly stance,
Nature's a jester, in a wild, joyful dance.

So let us skip through fields of delight,
Where laughter and blooms make everything right.
Join in the fun, you'll find it is real,
In these golden fields, life's a spinning wheel.

Golden Whispers

In a garden of gold, secrets unfold,
Whispers of laughter, both silly and bold.
The daisies debate on who's got the best,
While bumblebees snooze, dreaming of rest.

The sun says a joke, the shadows all cackle,
A squirrel in a hat starts to dance with a tinkle.
Petals break into giggles, can you believe?
Even the thorns wear a grin, don't deceive!

Oh! The ticklish breeze sends flowers in flight,
A daffodil teases a rose with delight.
They jive alongside rabbits, so spry and so sprightly,
Creating a scene, ever so lightly.

So shhh! Listen close to the giggling trees,
Nature's a comedian, with plenty of tease.
In this whimsical world, where laughter ensnares,
Golden whispers tell tales, light as the air.

Petals in the Dawn

Petals unfurl in the morning glow,
Dancing with laughter, putting on a show.
The sun winks at clouds, they puff up with pride,
As flowers spin tales, they giggle and glide.

In lighthearted mornings, the bee gets a thrill,
He buzzes a tune, his heart full and still.
A butterfly shimmies, trying to impress,
While daisies gossip, dressed in their best.

A flower's grand plan—a capital jest,
To wear mismatched petals, they think they look best!
The tulips all chuckle, they can't keep it in,
Their laughter erupts, like a mischievous grin.

So here's to each dawn, with petals galore,
Where humor blossoms and spirits can soar.
Embrace all the giggles, the blooms, and the fun,
In this garden of joy, every day's just begun.

Gilded Thoughts

In a garden, a flower wears gold,
Its petal dance has stories untold.
But bees come buzzing, oh what a surprise,
Stealing the nectar right before our eyes.

The sun hangs low with a wink and a grin,
Chasing away worries, letting joy in.
While the shadows stretch long, they play hide and seek,
As the wind tells tales with a little squeak.

Oh, can you believe this flower's grand show?
Twirling 'round bright while the squirrels steal the glow.
With laughter that echoes in every bright hue,
Nature's absurdities give us laughs anew.

So here in this patch where the silly convene,
We dance with the petals, all marigold sheen.
Why not laugh along as life's little jest,
In gilded thoughts, we are truly blessed.

Fields of Warm Ambiance

In fields where the gold blooms sparkle and play,
Grasshoppers boast in a very bold way.
They sing to the flowers, a humble brigade,
With poetic hops that may seem like a charade.

The wind whispers secrets to daisies nearby,
As the clouds drift by with a knowing sigh.
"I dare you to catch me!" the breeze seems to say,
"While you chase butterflies, I'll run away!"

Sunshine giggles, tickling all in its path,
While daisies and poppies plan a grand laugh.
The laughter is contagious, it spreads far and wide,
In fields where warm ambiance takes us for a ride.

So let's raise a toast to the petals that spread,
And the whimsical happenings, enough said!
We'll dance to the rhythm, though we're just passing through,
In the fields of pure joy, where happiness grew.

Saffron Serenade

Beneath a bright sun, the flowers all sway,
In a cheeky charade, they brighten the day.
A honeybee tipsy from sipping too sweet,
Dances with daisies in a wobbly beat.

The clouds wear smiles, casting shadows that creep,
While crickets and frogs share a laugh before sleep.
The tulips gossip, oh such silly tales,
Of snobby old roses and their pointy scales.

A pink flamingo struts like it owns the scene,
While dandelions giggle, "We're wild and we're green!"
It's a saffron serenade, vibrant and bold,
With colors so lively, they never get old.

So come join the chorus, let laughter take flight,
In the heart of the garden, everything's light.
With petals and breezes all ready to play,
We'll sway to the music of life's grand ballet.

Nature's Golden Canvas

A splash of yellow spills across the green,
Where creatures prance and giggle unseen.
The sun paints the world with a cheeky hand,
As if it has drawn its own funny band.

Lazy clouds float in a humorous race,
While shadows tease flowers with a tickling grace.
The ants march in line, a tiny brigade,
Mimicking soldiers in an odd masquerade.

Bees don their hats, looking smart in the air,
While butterflies twirl with extraordinary flair.
Amidst this canvas, colors collide,
In nature's own gallery, where laughter can't hide.

So stroll through this masterpiece, joy on display,
Join in the fun of this vibrant array.
With warmth in our hearts and smiles wide as the sea,
We savor the humor in life's jubilee.

Echoes of Summer

In fields where bees buzz loud,
A cat in shades takes a bow,
Sipping lemonade with flair,
Wearing sunshine in its hair.

The sunflowers twist and sway,
Doing the cha-cha all day,
While the kids run 'round like fools,
Chasing ice cream with big spoons.

Lawn chairs creak under the weight,
Of burgers grilled just to sate,
Flies join the party, hey-oh!
Sorry, buddy, you can't say no!

With echoes of laughter near,
Summer's jokes we hold so dear,
When the days seem extra bright,
Who knew fun could feel so light!

Blossoms of Joy

A garden blooms with giggles bright,
Petunias flirt with morning light,
Tulips tease with colorful flair,
Dancing with the cool spring air.

Bees in hats, quite a sight,
Sipping nectar, oh so polite,
While bunnies hop, with style they prance,
In this whimsical garden dance.

Weeds join in, thinking they're cool,
But they quickly learn the garden rules,
"No room for you," the flowers decree,
"Bouncing around, go bush or tree!"

But what's this? A sunflower sings,
As butterflies spread their wings,
In this flowery, funny show,
Joy blossoms where the laughter flows!

Embracing the Dawn

Wake up late, what a plight,
Coffee brews, oh what a sight,
Dawn creeps in with a cheeky grin,
Socks mismatched, let the fun begin!

Birds tweet tunes in off-key fun,
While the toaster pops—victory won!
The cat steals the cream, quite bossy,
As the dog barks, feeling frosty.

Sunrise spills in streaks of gold,
With a wink, the world unfolds,
Breakfast dance, cereal flies,
With pajama style—oh my, oh my!

Embracing each silly moment bright,
As the day begins in pure delight,
With laughter echoing all around,
In this quirky morn, joy is found!

Golden Inspiration

Golden rays through curtains stream,
A bright day's starting, what a dream,
Sketching ideas with splashes bold,
Inspiring tales yet to be told.

Butterflies flutter, they stop and stare,
At a pencil's line, creating flair,
A doodle here and a zigzag there,
Art's a mess, but who would care?

Coffee spills on papers strewn,
Marks of genius? Maybe soon,
As thoughts flop, like fish flailing,
In this madness, joy prevails, failing.

So chase your muse, let ideas flow,
In every slip, find room to grow,
For in the chaos, laughter thrives,
Golden inspiration, where joy arrives!

Golden Memories

In gardens bright, where laughter's sown,
Golden blooms with mischief grown,
They nod and giggle in the breeze,
Planting smiles beneath the trees.

Each petal whispers tales of yore,
Of picnic pranks and muddy war,
With bees that dance and butterflies,
Creating chaos in disguise.

The sunbeam's wink, the squirrel's chase,
A game of tags, a wild embrace,
As daisies plot a flower coup,
While tulips snicker, 'Look at you!'

In every color, mischief hides,
With rustling leaves, the fun abides,
So let us laugh, let worries cease,
In this bright garden, find your peace.

Dappled Sunlight

Under trees where shadows play,
Sunlight juggles, bright and spray,
The flowers giggle, colors bright,
Shy violets peek, then take flight.

A dappled dance begins to sway,
As bunnies hop, in pure dismay,
With every beam, a chuckle flows,
In nature's riddle, humor grows.

The daisies wear their cap of sun,
While bees buzz loud, just for fun,
Their tiny feet on nectar sip,
In this strange world, we all trip.

And as the grass hops around,
Each blade a tickle on the ground,
We laugh along, a sunny plight,
And skip together, wild in light.

Essence of a Flower

Oh, essence sweet, with scents so bold,
Your tales are funny, yet never told,
From daisies dressed in polka dots,
To roses boasting, 'Look at these spots!'

The lilacs gossip, soft and low,
While sunflowers wink, 'Let's steal the show!'
Their petals flutter, humor in air,
Like nature's jesters, beyond compare.

In every bloom, a chuckle found,
With bunny pranks all around,
The orchids chuckle in their bed,
While tulips tease, 'Who made that head?'

So dance, dear friends, in petals bright,
With laughter woven in the light,
For in each garden, joy takes flight,
As flowers tickle, all feels right.

Nature's Golden Artistry

In golden fields, there's fun galore,
Each bloom a hint of laughter's score,
While daisies play a game of tag,
And butterflies with grace just wag.

With every brush of nature's hand,
A canvas bright, a jester's land,
The ladybugs in polka spree,
Whispering secrets with glee.

The sun does paint in shades of bright,
And every flower shares delight,
So let's join in the merry play,
Where colors dance and jesters sway.

In this rich garden, joy's our art,
With chuckles sprouting from the heart,
So grab a petal, let's be spry,
In nature's joke, we all comply.

The Garden's Secret Song

In the garden, the flowers giggle,
While rabbits hop and do a jiggle.
Butterflies join in with a twirl,
As the bees buzz around in a whirl.

The daisies whisper jokes so sly,
While the sun peeks in, oh my, oh my!
Worms tell tales underground so deep,
While the daisies gather for a sleep.

Birds chirp laughs from up in the tree,
"Why did the scarecrow win?" you see!
"Because he was outstanding in his field!"
The garden's charm is surreal, revealed.

So here's to blooms with laughter wrapped,
In the sun's glow, we are happily trapped.
With secrets shared beneath the sky,
Together in joy, time flutters by.

A Dance of Sunlight

The sun's rays dip, then leap about,
Casting shadows with playful shouts.
The flowers sway in rhythm and cheer,
As their petals wiggle without any fear.

Grasshoppers in tails of green delight,
Join the party, leaping with might.
The daisies spin, then take a bow,
"Hey, let's not forget to dance now!"

Clouds drift by, sporting cottony hats,
Smirking down at the dancing cats.
"Why do they prance?" a pigeon crows,
"Because they've got rhythm, as everyone knows!"

Nature's tunes blend, a funky mix,
In this vibrant plot of floral tricks.
So raise a glass to the sunny ballet,
In the garden's warmth, we'll laugh and play.

Sunlit Reverie

Bright yellow blooms with cheeky grins,
Invite us to join their silly spins.
"Who wore it best?" they jest and tease,
While the bumblebees buzz with ease.

The sun drips gold on petals so bold,
The flowers gossip with tales untold.
"Did you hear about the wind that blew?
He thought he was cooler, but who knew?"

A ladybug spreads her polka-dots wide,
As butterflies flutter and take a ride.
"Is it hot in here, or just us?" they say,
In a whirl of joy, they dance and sway.

With every ray of sunlight's tease,
The garden holds secrets like a breeze.
In laughter's perfume, we find the way,
To cherish these bright, delightful days.

Luminous Days

The sun wakes up with a giant yawn,
Stretching across the dewy lawn.
It giggles as it spills out light,
While the flowers jump with sheer delight.

Leaves rustle, whispering jokes anew,
"Why did the tomato blush? It knew!"
Petals sway to the tune of glee,
As buzzing bees sip nectar with glee.

Gnomes laugh behind their shady hats,
Joining the fun with the chirping chats.
"What's the best part of a sunny day?
Flowers throwing petals at kids in play!"

Under the bright, luminous rays,
We bask in the wonders of our days.
With this playful dance, we come alive,
In the laughing camaraderie of nature's jive.

Radiance of the Sun

In the garden, bright and bold,
A flower's story yet untold.
It dances with a silly twirl,
Pretending it's the queen of pearl.

With petals wide and laughs so loud,
It tries to charm the passing crowd.
A bumblebee, it fools and flirts,
While wearing mismatched polka skirts.

The sunbeam whispers, 'What a sight!'
As daisies giggle with delight.
The tulips tease the shy, white rose,
"Come and join our joyful prose!"

In nature's stage, the flowers play,
In their own silly cabaret.
A bloom so bright, a jest so fine,
This sunny heart, forever shines.

Blossoms of a Dream

Once a petal tried to fly,
With a tiny leaf that said, "Oh my!"
Up it went, then down it fell,
"I'll try again," it rang the bell.

The breeze, it chuckled, swayed and spun,
As daisies joined the frolic fun.
"Are we flowers, or are we kites?"
Challenging the wind for silly fights.

Butterflies, in costumes bright,
Held a dance-off, what a sight!
With laughter shared upon the ground,
A garden full of joy was found.

Crowned in gold, they sang so loud,
Ignoring every passing cloud.
The blossoms tumbled, twirled, and gleamed,
Here's to a dream where flowers dreamed!

Echoes of Golden Hours

A sunflower stood with pride so tall,
Challenging the daffodils to a brawl.
"Who's the yellowest?" they did declare,
As bees buzzed round, without a care.

"It's not a race, just a bloom-off!"
The tulips laughed, they just can't scoff.
They swayed and sang, all in good fun,
As shadows stretched beneath the sun.

A garden of giggles, a field of cheer,
With every petal, spreading good near.
The evening's light turned soft and sweet,
As flowers shuffled, danced on their feet.

So here's to gold in every hue,
With laughter shared, they always grew.
In echoes bright, they find their way,
Silly flowers brightening the day!

Reflections in Yellow

In a pond, the petals play,
Making splashes, come what may.
"Look at us!" a lily shouts,
"Splashing colors, no more doubts!"

With quacky ducks, they join the scene,
"Is that your reflection, or just a bean?"
The roses giggle, their colors swirl,
"I'm the fairest here, not just a pearl!"

As dragonflies zoom by in style,
The garden bursts with endless smiles.
A flower's wink, a gentle tease,
The water ripples with giggling breeze.

In the sun's warm rays, they sway and swirl,
Creating laughter, a joyful whirl.
Reflections in yellow, colors divine,
In this funny bloom, everything's fine!

Threads of Sunshine Throughout the Year

Bright petals dance in the breeze,
Chasing thoughts like buzzing bees.
In gardens filled with giggles and cheer,
Who knew plants could be so dear?

Sunshine clothes the ground in gold,
Whispers secrets, tales untold.
Nature's jest, a playful tease,
A flower's grin, as sweet as cheese.

Laughter sprouts from every seed,
They grow like jokes—a joyful breed.
With every bloom, a wink is shared,
In this flower field, none are scared.

So lay down in the grassy knoll,
Breathe in the fun that fills your soul.
For every flower has its quirks,
In this garden of happy works.

The Color of Warm Embrace

A bloom that twinkles, bright and bold,
Wrapped in hugs of marigold.
The petals whisper secrets low,
As if they're in on the show.

In every laugh, a burst of hue,
Dancing sunlight, golden view.
The colors snicker, tease the sun,
In this garden, we all have fun.

With every petal, a joke is spun,
Like puns that weave and twist and run.
Life's little quirks in blossoms share,
Who knew flowers had such flair?

Let's paint the town with each new bloom,
Creating joy, dispelling gloom.
In laughter's garden, we shall play,
With warmth and cheer throughout the day.

Golden Trails of Memory

In a patchwork quilt of blooms so bright,
Memories twirl in the morning light.
Every petal has a story to tell,
As we wander through this floral shell.

Like breadcrumbs in the garden fair,
Each blossom's tale sings in the air.
Laughter echoes where flowers convene,
In vivid colors, life feels serene.

Oh, the giggles tied to roots so deep,
Where flower folk in sunshine leap.
They teach us joy, they teach us glee,
These little suns, wild and free.

So gather 'round, and take a seat,
In this fragrant world, oh so sweet.
For each flower carries a laugh so bright,
Creating memories in pure delight.

Dialogues in Floral Palette

The daisies chat with giggles and glee,
Sharing tales of a bumblebee.
Sunflowers nod in playful debate,
Their golden crowns, a jesting trait.

Roses roll their eyes in red,
While violets tease with words unsaid.
They weave a story, a comedy scene,
Where petals blush and laughter's keen.

In the garden where hues collide,
Egos bumble, blooms reside.
The flowers sport their brightest attire,
As they gossip near the fence they aspire.

Oh, let us join this floral chat,
A bouquet of laughter, how about that?
For in this tapestry, we find our fate,
In dialogues bright, we celebrate.

Beneath the Amber Skies

Beneath the amber skies, I spy,
A bee in a bowtie, oh my!
It zigzags in style, with flair in its flight,
Swapping gossip with flowers, pure delight.

Dandelions giggle, their heads held high,
While tulips are plotting a pie in the sky.
With petals that flutter like gossip on wings,
Who knew garden blooms could be such funny things?

A squirrel in shades jumps onto the scene,
Stealing nectar with moves too smooth to be gleaned.
The roses just blush, and the daisies all roar,
As laughter ensues, what a fun-filled lore!

In this meadow of gold, we gather to play,
Each flower a jest, banishing gray.
Underneath amber skies where the humor blooms free,
Life's laugh is the nectar that sweetens the spree.

The Language of Blooming Souls

Once upon a thyme, in a garden so bright,
Where blossoms could chatter from morning to night.
Petunias teased daisies, a sweet little prank,
As bees giggled softly, all dressed in sweet rank.

Sunflowers winked, their faces so bold,
While violets whispered conspiracies old.
The roses rolled over, said, "Let's play charades!"
So they acted out stories with petal-made shades.

A moonlit reveal where secrets take flight,
With crickets as critics, providing insight!
Each laugh in the breeze like a butterfly's dance,
Hansel and Gretel would envy this chance.

In this playful garden, where humor is gold,
Flowers converse in a language untold.
With blooms that can giggle, and petals that cheer,
Each day spills a story, so vibrant and clear.

Reflections in a Meadow's Heart

In a meadow's heart, reflections abound,
With flowers that giggle and dance round and round.
Buttercups gossip with daisies in tow,
While the wind tells a secret that only they know.

A lily dips low, pretends to be shy,
While dandelions scatter, their hopes in the sky.
Hummingbirds chuckle as they zip to and fro,
Trading wild tales like stars in a show.

And there by the pond, where the ripples play nice,
Lies a frog in a crown, claiming he's twice as wise.
He croaks out a joke that no one can hear,
But the smile on the lily says, "Oh, my dear!"

Through reflections and laughter, the meadow spins
round,
Where joy is the anchor, and humor is found.
In this riot of blooms, with petals that burst,
We learn that the lightness can quench any thirst.

A Symphony of Golden Blooms

In a symphony of blooms, the melody sways,
With sunflowers strumming their golden-filled rays.
The tulips set tempo, in colors so bright,
While daisies clap hands in the soft morning light.

A petal parade, where the fun never stops,
As pansies perform in their marvelous tops.
The lilacs hum softly, creating a tune,
Even weeds join the dance beneath the good moon.

A bumblebee choir buzzes out of tune,
While the roses just chuckle and wink to the moon.
Petunia, the maestro, conducts with a grin,
As blooms burst with laughter, let the giggles begin!

In this vibrant garden, laughter takes flight,
With nature's own symphony, hilarious delight.
So come join the fun, where the blooms sing and play,
In this boisterous garden, let joy lead the way!

The Canvas of a Summer Breeze

In fields where laughter blends with light,
The flowers dance in sheer delight,
A bumblebee forgets his gait,
As he leads a wobbly fate.

Paint splatters on a canvas bright,
Sunshine's strokes, a comical sight,
Birds chirp tunes in silly rhymes,
While squirrels plot their nutty crimes.

Chasing shadows, hiding in play,
Tickling the toes of all who stray,
With grassy curtains swaying wide,
Nature beckons, let's all slide.

So here's to breezes soft and sweet,
That carry tales of tiny feet,
The canvas spins, oh what a tease,
In summer's grip, we find our ease.

Saffron Dreams Amidst the Green

Saffron dreams swirl in the air,
While crickets plot their evening flair,
A frog in polka-dots does leap,
Claiming it's a nighttime creep.

Beside the pond, a tale unfolds,
Of vegetables turning bold,
The carrots giggle, the beets blush red,
While cabbages scheme mischief instead.

Fireflies blink with teasing grace,
Leading the way in a starry race,
The moon chuckles, a guardian bright,
As veggies twirl in pure delight.

Oh to dance in these vibrant dreams,
Where nature laughs and laughter beams,
Saffron spice, oh what a green,
In funny realms, let's all convene.

Luminous Strands of Nature

In twilight hours, the fibers glow,
Nature spins tales, slow and low,
A spider all dressed in its finest wear,
Declares it's a fashionista affair!

With daisies draped in sunlight's gold,
And lazy breezes feeling bold,
Butterflies flit like little jesters,
Announcing the bloom of all the besters.

Oh, the oak tree winks, in leafy cheer,
While ants march on, full of fear,
The fireflies glow like winking eyes,
As nature crafts its bright disguise.

So laugh along, in this tangled play,
With luminous strands to light the way,
In every giggle, we find our glee,
In nature's web, let laughter be free.

Conversations with the Sun

Oh Mr. Sun, why shine so bright?
Are you trying to start a daylight fight?
With cheeks of orange and golden eyes,
You make the clouds all giggle and rise.

The daisies shout, with cheers so bold,
To share their stories of secrets untold,
"Catch us if you can!" they call with glee,
As the warm rays spark a daydream spree.

While shadows stretch to play their part,
A dance of whispers, a beating heart,
The world awakes to sunlit pranks,
Planting smiles in nature's ranks.

So here's to chats with that bright ball,
Full of promise, joy, and all,
A sunny jest, a playful pun,
Let's laugh together, just you and the sun.

Meadow Meditations

In the meadow, cows dance with glee,
A chicken in a hat claims the tea.
Grasshoppers play banjo under a tree,
While daisies gossip, so carefree!

Bees wear sunglasses, sipping on brew,
Telling tall tales of flowers they flew.
The sun's golden rays bid a cheeky adieu,
As worms in tuxedos plan their debut.

Ladybugs rollerblade, zooming by fast,
While butterflies cheer them on with a blast.
A snail with a suitcase, no need to be last,
Says, "I'll see you later!" and leaves in a cast.

With laughter and chatter, the meadow is bright,
Where clovers get tipsy on the warm light.
Join the frolic, oh what a sight!
In this land of whimsy, all feels just right.

Saffron Dreams

In saffron fields, the bees play prank,
Hiding the nectar in a gold tank.
Fluffy bunnies gossip, what do you think?
As tulips giggle, blushing in pink.

The sun wears flip-flops, taking a stroll,
While daisies debate who'll take the poll.
Worms in shades are watching it all,
With sparks of humor they can't control.

A cheeky crow plays tricks on a cat,
While frogs in a choir sing, "Ain't that fat?"
Saffron dreams on a lazy mat,
Where every silly whim is where it's at.

In laughter we find, joy blooms so bright,
Beneath the saffron, everything's light.
Join the fun under the fading light,
In fields of dreams, all feels just right!

Enchanted Petals

In enchanted gardens, the flowers conspire,
Telling jokes that never seem to tire.
A rose tells a secret to a wild briar,
While tulips giggle, lifting spirits higher.

Butterflies wear capes, flapping with flair,
A daffodil's dance is beyond compare.
Bumblebees hum a tune in the air,
As daisies roll laughter without a care.

The soil's got jokes that make worms turn red,
While petals plot mischief under the shed.
Squirrels play charades, by sun rays they're led,
In this charming world where fun is widespread.

Even the shadows dance with delight,
As the moon peeks in, glowing softly at night.
In enchanted petals, oh what a sight,
Where laughter and joy take wonderful flight.

Sweet Aura of Dawn

At dawn, the sun tickles flowers awake,
Silly shadows prance, making them shake.
While roosters recite poetry, for goodness' sake,
The blossoms all giggle, oh what a break!

Chirping birds host a morning chat,
As a sleeping hedgehog dreams of a hat.
A wily fox sneaks in, being quite fat,
In this sweet aura, laughter's where it's at.

Sipping on dew, the petals discuss,
Whispers of humor in a lively fuss.
While the early worms ride the bus,
Making merry should always be a plus.

As sunlight spills gold across the dawn,
The world's silly shenanigans never are gone.
In this sweet aura, let's all carry on,
Embracing the laughter 'til the day is drawn.